I READ!
YOU READ!

Child's Turn to Read   Adult's Turn to Read

WE READ ABOUT THE

Mayor

Stephanie Gaston
and
Madison Parker

Table of Contents

SEAHORSE
PUBLISHING

Parent and Caregiver Guide

Reading aloud with your child has many benefits. It expands vocabulary, sparks discussion, and promotes an emotional bond. Research shows that children who have books read aloud to them have improved language skills, leading to greater school success.

I Read! You Read! books offer a fun and easy way to read with your child. Follow these guidelines.

Before Reading

- Look at the front and back covers. Discuss personal experiences that relate to the topic.
- Read the *Words to Know* at the back of the book. Talk about what the words mean.
- If the book will be challenging or unfamiliar to your child, read it aloud by yourself the first time. Then, invite your child to participate in a second reading.

During Reading

 CHILD Have your child read the words beside this symbol. This text has been carefully matched to the reading and grade levels shown on the cover.

 ADULT You read the words beside this symbol.

- Stop often to discuss what you are reading and to make sure your child understands.
- If your child struggles with decoding a word, help them sound it out. If it is still a challenge, say the word for your child and have them repeat it after you.
- To find the meaning of a word, look for clues in the surrounding words and pictures.

After Reading

- Praise your child's efforts. Notice how they have grown as a reader.
- Use the *Comprehension Questions* at the back of the book.
- Discuss what your child learned and what they liked or didn't like about the book.

Most importantly, let your child know that reading is fun and worthwhile. Keep reading together as your child's skills and confidence grow.

Mayor

CHILD

A mayor leads the **government** of a city.

CITY HALL

3

In some cities, the people vote for their mayor.

Many cities elect a mayor every four years.

CHILD

In some cities, a city council decides who will be mayor.

ADULT

States have different rules about who can be mayor of a city in that state.

CHILD

In some states, you must be at least 18 years old to be mayor.

In some states, you must live in the city where you want to be mayor.

ADULT

Many **local** governments have a mayor and a city council.

CHILD

Mayors may lead the city council.

ADULT

Members of the city council are elected to make laws and rules for the city.

The mayor **approves** new laws.

CHILD

It is the mayor's job to **enforce** the rules and laws of the city.

ADULT

The mayor is in charge of **departments** in the city government.

CHILD

The police department and fire department keep people safe.

ADULT

The education department manages city schools.

CHILD

The transportation department keeps buses and subways running.

ADULT

The mayor helps during emergencies and natural disasters.

CHILD

Floods and wildfires are examples of natural disasters.

ADULT

The mayor holds meetings that are open to the people of the city.

CHILD

People can tell the mayor their ideas for making the city better.

ADULT

Francis X. Suarez was elected Mayor of Miami, Florida, in 2017.

CHILD

Lori E. Lightfoot was elected Mayor of Chicago, Illinois, in 2019.

ADULT

Francis X. Suarez
Mayor of Miami, Florida
elected 2017

Lori E. Lightfoot
Mayor of Chicago, Illinois
elected 2019

The mayor has an important job.

CHILD

The mayor is a leader who makes sure that people are following local laws.

ADULT

Words to Know

approves (uh-PROOVZ): officially accepts a plan or idea

departments (di-PAHRT-muhntz): parts of a government that have specific purposes and responsibilities

enforce (en-FORS): to make sure that a law or rule is obeyed

government (GUHV-urn-muhnt): the system by which a country, state, city, or other organization is run; the group of people who govern

local (LOH-kuhl): having to do with the immediate area where you live; close to your home

Index

Comprehension Questions

1. In some states, you must be at least _____ years old to run for mayor.
   a. 18
   b. 25
   c. 50

2. The mayor is in charge of _____.
   a. the city's police and fire departments
   b. the city's education and transportation departments
   c. all of the above

3. **True or False:** The mayor approves new city laws.

4. **True or False:** The mayor works with the city council.

5. **True or False:** Many mayors are elected every ten years.

Written by: Stephanie Gaston and Madison Parker
Design by: Jen Bowers
Editor: Kim Thompson

Library of Congress PCN Data
We Read About the Mayor / Stephanie Gaston and Madison Parker
I Read! You Read!
ISBN 979-8-8873-5628-0 (hard cover)
ISBN 979-8-8873-5629-7 (paperback)
ISBN 979-8-8873-5630-3 (EPUB)
ISBN 979-8-8873-5631-0 (eBook)
Library of Congress Control Number: 2023902907

Printed in the United States of America.

Photographs/Shutterstock: Cover and interior background circles ©
magic pictures, cover images ©2013 Monkey Business Images, ©2015
f11photo; p.3 legal pad ©2013 Mega Pixel, ©2021 Sheila Fitzgerald;
p.4 © 2016 AntonSokolov; p.5 ©2017 stock_photo_world; p.7 ©
Fourleaflover; p.9 ©2017 stock_photo_world; p.11©2018 create jobs
51, © Aquir; p.12 © patrimonio designs ltd, ©2015 a katz; p.13 ©2012
Josef Hanus, ©2017 Mikbiz; p.14 ©2019 Matt Gush; p.15 ©2018
24Novembers, ©2021 mkfilm; p.17©2020 Aaron of L.A. Photography;
p.19 Public Domain/City of Miami/www.miamigov.com, Lori Lightfoot/
Courtesy of the Mayor; p.20 © Vladvm; p.21 ©2018 YP_Studio

Seahorse Publishing Company

www.seahorsepub.com

Published in the United States
Seahorse Publishing
PO Box 771325
Coral Springs, FL 33077